The Silent Twin

CW00401759

A Haunting Tale Of Bonded Silence And Dark Secrets of June And Jennifer Gibbons

By

Clair Patterson

TABLE OF CONTENT

June and Jennifer Gibbons, often known as the Silent Twins, have a remarkable story that demonstrates the power of sisterhood and the importance of communication in our modern world. Although these two identical twins practically shared a lifetime in Wales and spoke a language that no one else understood, they were able to maintain written contact with the rest of the world. Almost immediately, the media began covering their strange relationship, and their strange story would soon capture the attention of people all around the world.

The story of June and Jennifer Gibbons, told in "The Silent Twins," is one of tragedy. The sisters and their parents emigrated to Wales from the Caribbean, where they were the only people of color. Due to being the target of school bullying and social exclusion from an early age, they isolated themselves and stopped interacting with others. They created a complex fantasy world for themselves as a means of escaping their reality. Concerned by the girls' actions, school administrators in Britain diagnosed them with mental illness and made attempts to isolate them. Their stubbornness as children led to their placement in a secure mental health hospital for treatment.

CHAPTER ONE

Prologue

In the early 1970s, Jennifer, young June, and Wales do not venture out of their bedrooms for the duration of the day. They will be cut off from all family members, including parents and siblings. They're pretty similar to one another in that they both have a fairly light dinner. Their normally quiet temperament drastically shifts when they are with themselves. Using an unusual form of cryptophasia, the girls communicate and keep journals. They make the universe a place where people, dogs, and parrots all coexist. When teachers are having trouble getting students to speak up, they may resort to a number of strategies. The girls are separated and placed in various foster care facilities and boarding schools. They are perpetually on the lookout for ways to hurt and escape themselves. The authorities have decided to confine the group in a single location.

In 1981, June and Jennifer started acting like typical preteens. They fall for the local bad guy, Wayne

Kennedy, and fixate all their attention on him. They break into his family's house to steal his clothes. Wayne's parents catch them, but at least they get to meet their son. Wayne initiates them into the exciting world of chemical sniffing and sexual encounters. However, the bullying got worse during their senior year of high school, and they turned inward and toward each other, experimenting with alcohol, drugs, and boys before committing a series of misdemeanors that landed them in prison for a combined twelve years at the notorious maximum-security Broadmoor hospital for the criminally insane. The twins were split up so that they could be reintegrated into society more easily. The strategy, however, backfired, and they became even closer than before.

They start bickering about how he really feels about them. Moreover, Jennifer starts to feel jealous of June's writing skills. Hallucinations brought on by drugs have been linked to serious acts of vandalism and crime. The judge hands down an extremely harsh sentence. Broadmoor is a gloomy psychiatric institute where they will be held indefinitely. The girls are miserable until a reporter named Jodhi May starts writing about their plight.

Let's not jump the gun; instead, let's go back to the very beginning...

CHAPTER TWO

Birth of the Twins

June Alison and Jennifer Lorraine Gibbons were born on April 11, 1963, in a hospital run by the Royal Air Force in the city of Aden in the Middle East. Though Jennifer arrived ten minutes later than June at 8:10 a.m., June seemed to be the more robust of the two due to her increased alertness and general better health. Their father, Aubrey, was tall, beautiful, and strict, while their mother, Gloria, had lovely eyes that gave her a sensitive and loving impression. The twins and their three older siblings were raised by their Barbadian parents in a tiny Welsh village in the 1970s and 1980s. They faced constant bullying at school and social marginalization from their neighbors because they were the only black family in the neighborhood. Still, they never shared anything beyond private conversations with one another. They wanted to escape their problems at home by chronicling their fantasies and tragedies in the Christmas diaries they had received, which ultimately sparked an interest in creative writing and a desire to pen their own novels.

West Indians who immigrated after World War II are often referred to as "the Windrush generation." This swell is so-called because it was named after the ship that transported many people from dark islands to the "mother country." The Gibbons family was of that era. And like every other immigrant, Aubrey and Gloria hoped that, once settled in Britain, they would become true Britons, replete with a stable family life and a deep appreciation for the Queen and cricket that they had learnt about at school. They also wished they could play cricket. They envisioned themselves putting down roots on a lovely section of the land and starting a family there. Instead, they moved from one posting to the next, constantly trying to blend in with a society that often found them repulsive or, at best, annoyingly different because of their strange accents, dark skin, and hair of an unusual texture. Because of their appearance, they also had a hard time getting hired.

The family relocated from Aden to the Royal Air Force installation in Linton, which is in the English county of Yorkshire, before the end of 1963. Gloria's twin daughters, whom she called "twinnies," were adorable with their rosy cheeks, hair bows, and bright grins. In 1967, they were blessed with the arrival of their little sister, Rosie. However, even as young children, they had trouble communicating; their sentences rarely exceeded four syllables. When his twins were eight years old, Aubrey packed up his family and moved to Chivenor in Devon. The girls were harshly criticized for the color of their skin and their resolve to remain silent when they first started attending their new school. They were probably eight or nine years old when the pain started, and by the time it was through, they no longer spoke to one another. After that, the twins avoided establishing eye contact, perhaps to protect themselves from the harsh judgments of others.

And after earlier responding to questions from their parents and older siblings, they cut off contact with them. "We reached a mutual understanding," June said, "we vowed not to speak with anyone." There were times when Aubrey and Gloria could hear the girls whispering in their room, but they understood their quiet better than the patois they used to communicate with each other.

CHAPTER THREE

High School

When Aubrey was deployed to Haverfordwest in 1974, the twins were eleven years old, and their family moved to a small house on an R.A.F. personnel housing estate. The awful acts of discrimination that took place in Haverfordwest made the city notable. At Haverfordwest County Secondary School, where the twins and their brother David were once again the only black students, the bullying was so bad that the girls had to be let out of school five minutes early every day to allow them time to get home before the worst of it started. They always seemed to leave school in lockstep with one another, one tall, slender girl leading the other with their heads lowered as if in prayer. In 1976, Haverfordwest invited school medical officer John Rees to town to vaccinate kids against TB. "The little Negress" stood before him, and he tried to inoculate her, but she seemed to be in a trance and was as dead as a doll. He gave her the vaccine, then rubbed some alcohol into her upper arm. A black girl who looked strikingly similar to her also had no reaction to the needle. Rees was worried and confused when he talked to the school's headmaster about it and the headmaster didn't seem to think the girls were especially distressed. The headmaster's reaction puzzled Rees, and he was appalled by their behavior. In other words, they did not create any problems, which was the main criterion used to evaluate the conduct of black students at the time. Evan Davies, the consultant child psychiatrist in the area, took over the case that Rees had referred to him. Davies made an effort to communicate with the twins but got no reaction. To quote what he had to say to Rees: "Treatment under these circumstances is a significant challenge that I am hesitant to accept." He instead recommended they attend Ann Treharne, the head speech therapist at Withybush Hospital in Haverfordwest, where they subsequently began therapy in February 1977. After Treharne left, they decided to read out loud and record it for posterity. Treharne listened to the CDs and concluded that the twins' "secret language" was actually a hybrid of English and Barbadian slang spoken at a high rate of speed. The girls' West Indian accents were influenced by the difficulty they had with palatal fricatives. They would, for instance, write "sh" for the letter "s." Treharne felt that June wanted to talk to her while Jennifer was there, and that Jennifer's eye motions were the only thing keeping them apart. It looked like Jennifer was in command of what June did.

The girls were recommended to attend the Eastgate Centre for Special Education in Pembroke, eight miles away, by Rees, Evans, and educational psychologist Tim Thomas, who was brought in to help with the Gibbons case. There, a trainer by the name of Cathy was on hand. The girls are now Arthur's responsibility. Rees was a contributor to the final outcome. Because they felt helpless to make decisions for their daughters, Aubrey and Gloria deferred to British officials, who were said to have more competence and knowledge than they did.

The girls' academic performance improved slightly at Eastgate compared to their previous institutions. Even after seeing therapist Tim Thomas, they continued to respond to each other with the same stiffness and gloomy faces that had previously spoiled family dinners. At these celebrations, their quiet reigned supreme, reducing their older sister Greta to tears on a regular basis. In 1977,

Thomas and Arthur suggested to their bosses that their two 14-year-old female employees be separated. June would be transferred to the adolescent unit at St. David's Hospital, located 30 miles from Eastgate, while Jennifer would stay at Eastgate.

CHAPTER FOUR

Eastgate

The two of them, Thomas and Arthur, just couldn't figure out how to treat it. The Eastgate team was divided on this method, which was harsh but presumably meant to help the twins establish their individual identities. Thomas's job was to explain the plan to the ladies. The twins were terrified of the prospect of being separated, despite their prior flirtation with the idea (for example, they would periodically write notes pleading for one of them to be sent to

Barbados and the other to America).
Minutes later, they were yelling at
each other and punching and kicking
each other. Using her fingernails,
Jennifer scraped June's cheek in an
aggressive manner. At one time, June
ripped all of Jennifer's hair out of her
head. They had to be forcefully
separated after they yelled at each
other and tried to push each other
out of Thomas' office.

Suddenly, they could or would
express themselves verbally. They
talked to Thomas and a lot of their

other Eastgate coworkers, promising to keep in touch if they were allowed to stay together. In March of 1978, the divorce was finalized. June's melancholy was already really bad when she got to St. David's, but it got so bad that she virtually stopped moving while she was there. Two people were needed to take her out of bed, and once they did, they could only lean her against the wall. As far as "rehabilitation" goes, it's safe to say that the breakup was a bust. Both sisters had dropped out of school for good and were working the dole by the winter of 1979, prompting June's return to Eastgate. They were both 16 years old then. When they returned home, the twins ate in their room, which was furnished with bunk beds and a window that looked out onto the street. They used to dine in the common area, but the smell of food persisted in their room, so they stopped. Except for their younger sister Rosie, they never spoke to anyone else. They wrote things down such, "We want to watch 'Top of the Pops' tonight at 7:00 p.m." when they needed to coordinate something.

Please don't lock the family room door. It was obvious that Aubrey had long since given up on trying to blend in, despite the fact that he never said as much. When he got home from work, he'd put on a show to pass the time until Gloria was ready to make dinner. After all, he was "just colored," his work was relatively low-stress, and his two children had left him. Just what was he trying to convey? David had already departed. Greta rarely dropped by the house. June knew her parents were suffering and confused, but she couldn't bring herself to accept it. On that particular occasion, she wrote, "I worry about my mum" in her journal. I can see the pain of our long relationship in her eyes. She's not a spring chicken, but she's got all the charm and naiveté of a young girl. Due to the length of time the twins and their parents were apart, both sets of parents felt as though they had lost touch with their children.tend to be content when accomplishing very little. As one teacher put it, "They lack initiative and inventiveness." The teacher was wrong; the students used their imaginations to change not only themselves but also their stifling classroom setting. They used dolls to recreate a new family to take the place of the one that had been shunned. Twins with unusual names like Johnny Joshua and Annemarie Esther Kingston, or Alma and Billy Hoe Haines, made up the vast majority of their doll offspring. Dolls were also used to represent the Gibbons family. Most of them were American; they came from places like Philadelphia and Malibu.

As part of a new "self-improvement" initiative, Gloria gifted red leather-bound diaries with locks to June and Jennifer for Christmas in 1979. Both girls began keeping extensive diaries. The crimson leather cover of the diary was secured with a lock on the front. They combined their financial aid and enrolled in a correspondence course in creative writing under the name of a single person using the phony student ID number 8201 to do it.

CHAPTER FIVE

The Manuscript of June

June's novel, "The Pepsi-Cola Addict," was started in January of that year. The novel's protagonist, Preston Wildey-King, is a young man from Malibu who often daydreams about leaving the area.

His abode was either too hot in the summer or too freezing in the winter. Since the day's heat was trapped inside, the room never cooled down enough to be comfortable. Preston thought he saw some signs of shivering. His stomach churned and his mind spun. It appeared to be icy. He reasoned that whether he was in Arizona or Hawaii, he wouldn't care what other people did because he would always be able to cool off with a nice drink. While he lounged around in his own apartment and drank 300 cans of Pepsi-Cola per day. The teacher starts to feel romantically invested in Preston. He has joined forces with a group of criminals. Then, while he is in jail, a homosexual inmate attempts to seduce him. Finally, after visiting his mom and sister, a finds a dead that appears to have been caused by a barbiturate overdose in their basement.

Both "The Pugilist," about a boy whose heart is failing and whose surgeon father decides to implant in him the heart—and soul—of their boxer dog, and "Discomania," about a group of urban youths who are controlled by their need for a disco beat, were written by Jennifer in a short period of time. Both of these books featured a child protagonist whose failing heart was to be replaced with an artificial organ implanted by the protagonist's surgeon father. On June 8, 1980, two months after her seventeenth birthday, she wrote in her diary, "Today I began writing my wonderful new novel, 'Discomania.'" The previous evening, she had stayed up late working on the fourteen tale segments. It will work, of that I am certain.

June convinced Jennifer to use her welfare funds to help publish June's work, but Jennifer's efforts to have her manuscript published by major publishing houses were unsuccessful. A vanity press published June, the novel. She spent days with June taking "author photographs," and she wrote at an incredible rate the entire time. They wrote the first draft of their journals, then revised and improved them until a final version fit for posterity was achieved. They wrote in their journals as if they were masterpieces of literature. June and Jennifer, both then aged 18, felt the tug of adulthood. They needed someone to notice them, so they went to see Lance Kennedy, a fellow student at Eastgate who had helped them out of a jam before. Though they couldn't have known it at the time, they had filed away memories of Lance regardless. Lance was an American citizen. By the time the twins located his childhood home in Welsh Hook, some 10 miles from Haverfordwest, he had relocated to Philadelphia. However, he still had three younger brothers, Jerry (the eldest), Wayne (around the same age as the twins), and Carl (the youngest), who were all still living in Wales at the time.

CHAPTER SIX

Juvenile Delinquencies

In April of 1981, June and Jennifer took their first taxi to the Kennedy residence. They found nothing unusual when they arrived. The entrance was only partially locked. They smashed a bedroom door, ate peanut butter sandwiches, examined clothing worn by the Kennedy sons, and viewed photographs of Hawaii on the walls. When the boys' biological father and stepmother arrived, they discovered the girls attempting to depart. However, the girl's biological parents felt awful for the twins and abandoned them when they could not coax them into speaking. June and Jennifer persisted in their efforts despite multiple failures. Using their remaining funds, they took taxis to Welsh Hook. Eventually, they met the remainder of the Kennedy boys and established regular contact. The ladies also learned about the negative effects of alcohol and other substances. Carl, the youngest Kennedy child at the time, saw potential in these strange black females in wigs and mismatched clothing. Carl's age was only fourteen. In June of 1981, Jennifer sent her letter. I can state with absolute certainty that today was one of the best days of my short life. Carl Kennedy is responsible for robbing me of my enchanting virginity. At least currently. Not enjoyable, but necessary nonetheless. There was considerable blood present. Naturally, during devotion. Lord, I apologize. A competent ally. Jenny."

June saw Jennifer and Carl having sex in a church chancel near the

Kennedys' home while all three were intoxicated.

There appears to be a supernatural element to the occurrences. Now, for the first time, I can see myself from Jennifer's perspective. She believes I am slow, frigid, harsh, and overly talkative, but she holds the same opinions of her. Both of us are impeding the development of the other. Her eyes exhibited a frigid, calculated expression. Oh my god, I'm genuinely terrified of her. She is clearly acting inappropriately. She is currently utterly inconsolable. Unknown individual threatens her sanity on a regular basis. I am alone.

Thirteen days after her sister's inebriated adventure, June attempted to reenact it by becoming intoxicated in the Kennedys' barn. As the young man fumbled and searched for her, she yelled, "I love you!" in a fit of despair and desperation. No woman had ever experienced a romantic or erotic encounter. It was their summer, despite the Kennedy boys' disregard, insults, and physical assault. It was the first summer they spent as actual persons as opposed to dolls, and they filled their room with journals and manuscripts. They lacked a basis for comparison because they had never spent much time with males before. There was nothing mysterious about the Kennedy siblings' looks. The Kennedys treated the twins as two puppies begging at their feet for attention and food leftovers, which they occasionally gave them. Family members scarcely tolerated the Kennedys' presence. Before returning to the United States at the conclusion of the summer, the Kennedy daughters desired to bring something to remind them of their summer spent in Europe. Carl presented them with a soiled T-shirt, Jerry with a picture and two mismatched pairs of socks, and Wayne with an outdated parka. Fall, 1981. Since they had no one else to blame for their grievances, the twins directed their anger toward themselves. They had expended all of their money on food. They continued to consume and purge, which only served to make their lives more monotonous and routine. They documented their emotional and mental distress in detailed and candid diaries. When the twins viewed each other in the mirror, they saw a reflection of their own distinct brand of nothing. They sought to improve their appearance by purchasing and acquiring West Indian hair and skin products. They investigated the supernatural. Jennifer penned, "I am now directing currents of my higher psychic mind to instruct my guardian angel to work via my skin and contact my healing skills in order to remove the scar on the bridge of my nose." Jennifer described the lesion located on her nasal bridge. But until they worked out who they were for one another, they could not determine who they were meant to be for everyone else.

June's email stated, "J. and I have a romantic relationship, and our connection is marked by a lot of love and a lot of rage at times. Apparently, I am a coward in her eyes. She has no comprehension of how much she adds to my anxiety. I've never felt more frail than I do now. I must be able to place some space between my emotions and hers. I no longer believe in humanity, please, Lord. In an interview, Jennifer stated, "She should have died at birth." Because Cain murdered Abel. No one will be able to forget about it. According to June, "I am in captivity to her, this creature that is with me every hour of my life." Jennifer: "I don't believe J. to be my twin. My actual twin was born at the same time as I was, appears identical to me, possesses the same personality traits as I do, desires and pursues the same goals, and even has the same ascending sign as I do. This individual will be aware of my shortcomings, errors, and prejudices. There are no disparities; everything results in identical twins. I cannot tolerate individuals who differ from me.

As time went on, they expanded their hatred to include the natural world. After being turned down by a local gang, the two decided to strike out on their own. They started breaking into people's houses, taking bikes and glue among other things. Additionally, while at the location, they broke into a nearby school. The adult training center was designed to help those who suffer from spasticity. They smashed windows, stole books, and spray-painted offensive messages all over the building. They tried to smash a payphone, called 9-1-1 to report it, and then ran away before police could arrive. Eventually, the siblings grew bored with their achievements and sought new challenges. June said in an email, "I want to build gasoline bombs." I'm going to throw a bottle, some gas, and some papers in there. The most notorious arsonist in the area is going to be me! The fire consumed, destroyed, and cleansed as if embodying their anguish and hope all at once.

The twins shattered a window at Pembroke Technical College on November 8th. A neighborhood patrol officer followed them after hearing them, calling for backup. They ended up being arrested. Diaries detailing break-ins and fires were found when their room was searched.

Two days later, the twins were transferred to the Pucklechurch Remand Centre, which is located about sixteen kilometers outside of Bristol. Seven months passed while the legal system deliberated what should be done with the twins.

It appears the twins' social seclusion was the result of their own stubbornness rather than their terrible circumstances. There were sporadic attempts at self-improvement, such when one of them enrolled in a correspondence course called "The Art of Conversation," but the results were usually superficial. The tenacity of the people responsible for them mirrored their own dogged resolve.

The close bond that developed between the twins during their time at Pucklechurch jail ended up causing them pain. Neither could stand being in one other's presence, whether physically or mentally. They had been separated for so long that they had grown to wish for each other's deaths. The only time they were ever in the same room together was when they plotted each other's deaths. They were both so lonely and unhappy apart that they considered ending their lives. Then, after being reunited, they were disheartened by being told their strength actually lay in their time apart.

CHAPTER SEVEN

Trial and Conviction

The sisters faced 16 counts of burglary, theft, and arson at their trial in May of 1982. They listened to their lawyers and pleaded guilty, which led to an indeterminate sentence of incarceration at Broadmoor. Broadmoor had been the subject of the girls' imaginations for weeks, ever since the doctors had portrayed it to them in words more fitting of an English Eden than a jail hospital.

June went into a trance a few days following the birth of her twins and their arrival at the hospital. A couple of weeks later, she made an unsuccessful suicide attempt. Jennifer physically attacked the nurse. Patients were placed in different wards and ordered to avoid contact with one another. When they first started working at Broadmoor, they were only 19 years old. Both girls hoped to settle down and have families of their own someday. It took June a whole month to finally open her mouth, and when she did it was usually to flash that unpleasant smile. Jennifer was met with doubt every time she tried to express her feelings and views. The antipsychotic medicine depixol was injected into her on a regular basis, blurring her vision and making it difficult for her to read and write. Antipsychotic medicine was increased in June.

Over the course of over a decade, inmates competed to see who could eat the most and flirted with male inmates. It had been years since the twins had any idea why they were still undergoing this "treatment." The doctors and social workers had initially thought the children could get by with another year or two, but after reviewing their situation on a more regular basis, they changed their minds. Sometimes Jennifer would feel so down that she would just collapse. Jennifer would continually apologize for starting fights with her sister whenever the two of them were confined to the same space, during which she repeatedly accused her sister of ruining her life.

The twins' long wait for release ended in March 1993, a month before they turned 30, when they were transferred to a clinic with a medium level of security.

Jennifer, who had been sick and listless, laid her head on her sister's shoulder during the bus ride to their new location. She remarked, "Finally, we're out of Broadmoor," as the gates closed behind them. There, despite her sister's best efforts, Jennifer went into a coma.

It was revealed that she had died that evening from undiagnosed acute myocarditis, a rare ailment that causes inflammation of the heart. Death is an extremely rare outcome.

The following year, June's parole conditions were lifted. She said she was "hysterical with grief" at first, but that going through it helped her find her voice, learn to live for her sister, and discover her strength.

END

Printed in Great Britain
by Amazon

43795920R00036